I Love You, But I Hate You, But I Need You

HOW TO LOVE UNCONDITIONALLY FOR SOMEONE LIVING WITH BORDERLINE PERSONALITY

Austen Lennon M.D.

CONTENTS

What Is Borderline Personality Disorder

Borderline personality disorder is an extremely serious mental disorder of impulsive actions and usually has a chain of unstable relationships. You can see the disorder with marks of ongoing mood instabilities and other instabilities such as behavior, self-image, and function. The person with BPD has very high anger, depression, and anxiety episodes that can last from a few hours to a few days. You can have BPD in correlation to having mood disorders, anxiety disorders, eating disorders, substance abuse, self-harm, suicidal thoughts, and suicide. Most medical professionals will agree with each other on the fact that the name "Borderline Personality Disorder" is misleading to the average citizen, but sadly a more accurate term does not exist yet.

There are many signs and symptoms of people with BPD, the most common that you will see is extreme mood swings. You can also see efforts to escape or avoid real abandonment or imagined abandonment. An unusual pattern of unstable relationships with your friends and family. It can sway from extreme closeness and love to hatred and anger. You will see them having a wrongly portrayed version of themselves or their self-image. You will also see many reckless behaviors such as spending outrageous amounts of money, abuse of substances, driving recklessly, and binging. Cutting and suicidal thoughts also show up in people with borderline personality disorder. Mood changes are regular with mood swings that last for a few hours to a few days. Many people with BPD observe a strong feeling of emptiness, uncontrollable anger, inappropriate comments, and having stress-related paranoid thoughts. Most people also feel cut off from themselves, as if they are observing themselves from outside of the body and slowly losing touch with reality. Any of these symptoms can be triggered by the minuscule events.

People with borderline personality disorder can see the anger in others while they are showing a neutral face and can also hear the anger in people's words more usually than people without BPD. Some of the symptoms above can also be traced back to other mental issues, and to people who don't have any mental issues, so do not just assume someone around you have this disorder and go get a doctor's diagnosis. A suitable medical professional needs to do a thorough assessment to see what outcome is appropriate.

1

Borderline personality disorder affects 5.9% of adults during one stage of their life. That equates to about 14 million Americans having BPD. You can see a connection of mental disorders within the patients with multiple diagnoses. About half of the people with Alzheimer's disease have borderline personality disorder. With others, like schizophrenia and bipolar disorders, are set around 2.25% of people. In psychiatric hospitals, about 20% of the patients are affected by it. In all outpatient treatments with mental health, BPD affects 10% of those patients. It is a theme to see this disorder around, possibly people you know could have it and no one knew. It seems like a small percentage because only 1 out of 20 people are affected you will still be around that 1. It is best to talk to your doctor if you have concerns beach being undiagnosed will hurt you especially with BPD. You need other's help to get more control of yourself, by treatment or by expressing all of those emotions. You can get past the spot that you are in now. Out professionals tell you that if they are engaged in any type of treatment that they are trying to help better themselves, and that is all they need for a good outcome. You can't figure out everything on your own, you need a new perspective on it. You have been the only one analyzing your brain for all of these years so it will be a change to have another by your side doing the same. They care about you and the outcome you want to also get to. They will listen to whatever you have to say and they could even respond with something that opens a new pathway in your brain, something you have never really thought to do before but now you have heard it just looks so obvious. The benefits outweigh the negatives in this situation because it's worth it to have an improved life. You will start to feel more confident about yourself, you need to feel that self-love. Once you can see the good in you and at the same time control your crisis moments, you will be at peace with yourself.

2

Does Someone You Care About Have BPD

If you know someone with Borderline Personality Disorder than you will have better insight on this next chapter.If someone close to you, a friend or loved one, has BPD then you know it affects you too. If you care about this person then you will need to help them find the proper providers and medications for treatment. You need to be there for them, just in case they have the wrong diagnosis or need assistance. Show lots of support with their decision to stick to the current treatment or to seek better treatment out there.

Your friend could use someone there with emotional support. You need to comfort that inner side of them to help them stay positive. Understand to your hardest what they are going through because it will never be enough in your eyes. Try your hardest to encourage them throughout life. Push them to thrive in every subject they challenge throughout the day.

You have already taken that first step towards helping your friend or relative, just by researching more in-depth about their disorder is enough. You should learn as much as you can about borderline personality disorder and any other mental disorders you can. The more you can learn about the mind and how it can be altered, the closer your loved one will feel to you. If you know why things happen the way they do with BPD then it will be a lot smoother of a ride. If you get written permission from your friend or loved one you can actually talk with his or her therapist to learn about different therapies that involve family members. You can also encourage your loved one with BPD to do family therapies.

One of your biggest responsibilities for caring for your loved one is to make sure that you never ignore any comments about someone with borderline personality disorder intent to harm himself or herself or even someone else. You should report these comments as soon as you hear them to the person's therapist or their doctor. If it is urgent enough and possibly life-threatening then you may need to call the police or just dial 9-1-1.

If you are at all curious about borderline personality disorder or you just want to feel closer to your loved one you should learn more about this. You can go to therapies specifically for significant others and they can teach you the information on it and how you can still be a part of their lives. It is a good idea if you are also wanting to learn about yourself more. You should be doing something like this if you are married to someone with borderline personality disorder. You can't just act like the problem is not there, it will never go away that way. You married someone that is a challenge, but will be rewarding in due time. You have to put in as much work as they are putting in themselves. You have to be a selfless person who can take a lot, someone who adores helping and is flexible. It is hard to stay together forever with someone who has BPD but it helps when you both are working towards better selves and a better relationship.

Your relationship with your close friend or loved one who has BPD will not change overnight because you went to therapy or because you started to care about the exchange of words more. You have to start building the house before you can decorate it. It will take time, months even years, but for some people, they need this so they can have some stable relationships. I will go into more detail in future chalets on how you can do all of that but I am not at all a therapist who understands and has studied these symptoms for years. Refer to them for further help if you truly want to help rebuild a hurt relationship. You will notice that even after years of you both learning how to treat each other in a relationship that you will have some slips and it all can break loose again. But that happens, no one is perfect. You will always have those emotions and you are just learning on how to tame them inside of you. So, days like those are always going to come and go, you just need to know what thoughts that pass through you should hold on to and the ones you should let in one ear and out the other. You need to know that not every emotion you feel on the inside needs to be brought out in this physical world. It is hard to pinpoint some emotion you are feeling because you feel them and you can't communicate with them.

Reasons like this are why I believe loved ones can help you just as much as your therapist. If you go to a therapist and your family does too, when you aren't around your therapist then that is the time to practice what they preach. Your family is there during those times to help you with what they were taught. They are the personal therapists you get to have for the rest of your day after your session. They can help you and you have to know that is all they want to do so never get upset when they are just trying.

If you are a significant other, loved one, or close friend who knows their friend or loved one has BPD and they aren't doing anything about it you should prepare something to tell them so you can help. They cannot do this on their own because they are stuck in their own minds, they need a therapist to bring them out of the box to see the world as it is. You need to come up to your friend or loved one with the most love and empathy you can have in you, and start the conversation off with ease. You obviously need to research all of this before you go at them for not doing anything positive to help.

The best way to bring it up is to keep reassuring them that you love and care about them so much that's why you are doing this.

3 How People Get BPD

Most mental disorders are still being figured out to this day. People are learning new things with the technology we have. Sadly, the cause of some mental disorders, including BPD, aren't completely understood. From what we understand about borderline personality disorder is that it might be caused by environmental factors or genetics. There have been studies shown with twins and with families that the link between BPD and the person with it is their family's history. They could have inherited them from a family member or it could be very strongly associated with any other mental disorder that they are diagnosed with. Other research has shown that the people that carry BPD also could have some brain abnormalities. Studies have been done and they can see the changes in aggression, impulsiveness, and regulating your emotions. Also, in function with that, certain brain chemicals may not function as well as others. Mostly the chemical is serotonin.

There are a few risk factors for people to be a predisposition for this disorder. The way your personality develops can be a fraction of the reason why you are the way you are. There is always going to be hereditary links within your family. If your close relative has this disorder or a similar linked disorder, you could be prone to it at birth. That isn't always the case though, there have been many people with borderline personality disorder that report they have been sexually or physically abused even neglected during childhood. Those years are your most important years, they are the building blocks to the beginning of your life. You can also have had some experiences being lost and/or separated from your guardian. That pulls you closer to the abandonment that you will always feel even when it's not there. Every incident in your life has changed you into you. Even just watching and experiencing your guardian do heavy substance abuse, especially if they have a mental disorder of their own. Family relationships affect you so much when you are growing up, the more native the more negative down the line you will feel about life.

Any hostile or just unstable ties in your family are not good to have. As a child, you don't really understand what is right and wrong when your parents do things because you assume that they are the all-knowing parents. You think whatever your parents are doing to you is what is happening to everyone around the world, you think of your reception as everyone's perception. That's why at this age you need to be in a healthy and stable household. If you are genetically inclined to BPD then you should have your family be your support, not your punching bag.

Even your own personality traits that you have built upon yourself can affect your mental state. Some personality traits linked to borderline personality disorder are anger, aggression, and impulsivity. In your mind, you have a garden, a garden of all your emotions. The emotions you feed and water the most will grow the tallest, the ones you give into start to take over. You need to learn how to evenly spread out your water because you can't let your anger and aggressiveness be the pilot of your life. You can fly the plane pretty well by yourself.

If you are an outsider wanting to learn more about this disorder and how you can help a loved one then you can also see the signs of when they are falling off the rails. Usually, you know when the BPD has taken over but you truly need to see the full circle of why they are the way that they are. If you see your loved one constantly changing their job or just being fired, you should talk to them. Let them know how great you see them, and how they aren't alone. If they don't complete their education or just drop out, see why. You can always push them to do things that they probably didn't think they could accomplish or it could just be a nice conversation about why they didn't like the schooling there were getting. If they are getting into constant legal issues, especially jail time, then talking to them will help get feeling off their chest that they probably didn't say out of their head until that moment. If your relationship with them is straining or you see their personal relationship filled with constant conflict then you can always step in to help. If it's not your relationship, then don't give any tips and tricks for their significant other. Just tell them that they can do so much to help their relationship with therapies made for spouses of BPD patients or taking time to learn about themselves. You don't want to interject into someone's relationship but you can always help push them into making their own decisions that will help them in the end.

If it is your relationship then just do everything I said up there for yourself. You can take some time out and figure out you and why you both work together. Having therapy helps too, you can do family therapy with your whole family so you all can be comfortable with talking to each other emotionally, or you can do single therapy with a therapist who specializes in BPD loved ones. It's becoming a more common theme to have more therapies for this because it's becoming more of a widespread issue. You should always help them and see the person inside is trying. It's much harder for people with BPD to not just put emotion into everything they say. Some people with BPD can also be associated with another mental illness so you always need to know that anything can happen with them and that this is more of a struggle for them than it is for you. So, I know you can get through it.

The most common mental disorders to have in correlation with borderline personality disorder are alcohol or any other substance abuse, anxiety disorders, attention deficit or hyperactivity disorders, bipolar disorders, depression, eating disorders, and post-traumatic stress disorder.

4

How to Feel Empowered and Boost Your Confidence While Having BPD

It is very hard for people to boost up their self-esteem, but it is a million times harder for people with BPD. Self-esteem is the way we think about ourselves. If you have BPD, you could possibly have very low self-esteem and that can have a negative impact on your life. The stronger your self-esteem is the more time you can remain confident, strong, and easily connect with other people. If you have borderline personality disorder then feeling good about yourself is very rare, instead, you might feel underutilized or worthless more often. There are easy ways to build yourself up and be confident in the person you have blossomed into.

With BPD, you might be only able to assert your feeling and thoughts through anger. You need to learn how to work past that and express yourself calmly. You need to express how you are feeling without personal attack. It will take some time before your subconscious starts to understand this as well but by then I'm hoping communication will be a breeze.

It might help you see the good in yourself if you remember the good that people have seen in you in the past. Try to keep a little journal and write down every compliment that someone gives you. In the moment of writing it down you will get a great feeling and on your worst of days, that is a wonderful book to help brighten your mood.

You really need to focus on your positive qualities. You need to remember that every single person has those awful qualities that aren't as desirable but your overall goodness inside of you will always outweigh your negatives. You might only be able to name a couple positives on the top of your head but if you wanted to you can use that same journal and compile a list of everything you enjoy in yourself. I swear to you that list will just keep growing and growing the more you think. You truly are a gift to this world and seeing that in yourself is like heaven.

If you get those little voices in your head telling you how awful you are doing or that you are going to mess up then you should talk back to those voices and tell them they've got it all wrong. This is the one time in your life you need to talk back because those mental preparations before anything can change the entire outcome. Be positive in yourself and I swear it will all turn out positive in the end. How you treat and talk to yourself can make a huge difference in the outcome of any situation.

You need to also open up your eyes to the rest of the world because they are all worried about the same image you are putting up for yourself. Everyone is trying to learn that self-love and is thinking that everyone is talking about them. Ease up a little bit, we are all too into ourselves to be judging and talking about others. Just focus on yourself and you will see yourself growing. If by now you truly wanted that journal then here is another thing to write down in it; every evening, just write down all your accomplishments for the day. Everything you did that made you proud to be you or even just things you handled well. It doesn't have to be big, it could be just to remember to brush your teeth in the morning. Your brain makes notes of your successes and it encourages you to move towards those goals.

When it comes time to be confident, you may find yourself in your head, going over all of the worst-case scenarios that may come along with attempting to do whatever it is you are trying to do. It is important to keep in mind is that the only way you will ever be more confident is if you take the first step. If you find yourself still having trouble then the following tips might be useful.

Try and reframe your anxiety, if you are unsure about what the outcome of a certain event is going to be, that uncertainty can manifest itself as anticipation which can easily become fear with the right triggers. If you react in a situation where you would benefit from being self-confident with anxiety, you will lose the momentum you might have had going in the situation. Instead, you may find it helpful to react to anxiety as if it were curiosity instead. Rather than being anxious about what's to come, trick your mind into being curious about what is going to happen instead. If you can think of the experience as a type of experiment, you will gain a level of detachment from the situation that will make it much easier for you to power through in the long run. Curiosity and self-confidence go together much more easily than anxiety and self-confidence and you may find that curiously helps your confident momentum continue.

If that doesn't work, you might find success instead in taking the time to consider why it is that you are really afraid. If you find you always respond to similar instances that require self-confidence in a negative way you might need to take a look inside and consider why this is the case. It could be because your mind is finding patterns where no true pattern exists which may mean you are responding to stimuli as you perceive them, not the way the situation is actually presenting itself.

To combat this, the next time you start to feel nervous or scare before having to be self-confident, simply take an extra moment to consider the situation as it truly is and consider what it is about the scenario that is making you feel the way you do. If nothing specific comes to mind then odds are you are about to act based on false information, no matter how real it may have seemed at the time.

When you are just getting the hang of being more self-confident, you will likely experience moments where your mind throws up apparent roadblocks to your success. The most typical version of this involves some type of worst-case scenario that may occur if you take a predetermined course of action. While these scenarios are likely going to be extremely convincing in the moment, they are likely only going to be based on the dimmest version of reality and are likely going to have little bearing on what will actually happen which is why it is generally going to be better to just push forward with what you were planning to do and ignore them.

While may well be easier said than done, focusing on the fact that everyone has their own issues to deal with can make failing much easier to handle. All you need to do is tell yourself that what might seem like the end of the world to you, is likely just everyone else's Tuesday. While it may be hard, try to keep in mind that failure alone is nothing to be ashamed of, and trying and failing once will likely make the second time much more manageable.

Consider what there is to learn from the current situation, even if you fail. If you stop focusing on how you are going to be embarrassed if you fail, you may realize that there wasn't that much to worry about, to begin with. Without the added pressure, you may even find that you succeed. What's more, if you stop focusing on the failure and start focusing on whatever it is you are doing and maybe actually learn from your mistakes.

When trying to find the nerve to do something you have never done before, you may find that it helps if you just consider the odds. It's like the lottery says, you can't win if you never play. If rather than running every time an opportunity to show self-confidence shows up, you instead make an effort to take full advantage of the situation you will find that over time, you will succeed at least as often as you fail. What's more, you will find that slowly but surely being self-confident may actually become a habit.

What you really just need to do is stop thinking about all the ways that you are going to try and be more self-confident in the future, and instead start focusing on how you can improve your interactions with others in the present. Remember, all the good intentions in the world won't amount to much of anything if you don't put them into practice once in a while. While stretching out of your comfort zone will naturally be difficult at first, the fact that it is just as difficult for everyone else should do something to bring you a little comfort. Don't forget, the only difference between you and the people you admire for their self-confidence is that they had the determination to take the first step towards self-improvement.

If, after considering these tips and suggestions you just don't see yourself being a pillar of self-confidence, then you may be better off just faking it. While this might seem like a joke, you will be surprised at how effective faking confidence can actually be. For example, imagine an interaction with the most confident person you know. Now, imagine that same conversation except the other person was faking their level of self-confidence the entire time. It's a fact that the only difference between a conversation where you appear to have self-confidence, and a conversation where you actually have self-confidence is how you end up feeling on the inside. If you still aren't convinced, go ahead and try it once, you are sure to be surprised by the results. What's more, if you continue pretending long enough, eventually the act will be indistinguishable from reality, even to you. Until you get to that point, however, you may want to keep some of the following tips in mind.

First things first, think back to the person you thought of as the pinnacle of self-confidence in the previous example, when you are still learning to respond to things in the way that a self-confident person would, all you need to do is ask yourself what that person would do in whatever situation you happen to find yourself in. Don't be vague when you ask this question either, the more specific you can get the better. Consider the way the confident person moves, how they respond in conversation, the way they use their body language to really get their point across and what their speech patterns are like and then do everything in your power to act the same way.

One of the most important facets of appearing self-confident is changing the way you walk and stand. If you have self-confidence then you are going to naturally be more inclined to stand up straight with your shoulders squared. Those with low self-confidence, on the other hand, are more likely to slouch and slump when they talk. To project a more self-confident image, then, all you need to do is make a point of assuming the correct posture whenever talking to others, don't forget to always look them in the eye as well. Those with high levels of self-confidence also always walk as if they have someplace that they need to be because they are important and so is their time. If you want to look more confident than you feel, simply adopting a walking speed that is about a fourth faster than average should start to make a noticeable difference on the way others perceive you.

If you think back to your self-confidence idol, you will likely realize that they tend to pay a lot of compliments to others. This is because they often feel so good about themselves that they can't help but share the love with those around them. As such, making a point of complimenting others more will naturally cause them to assume you are more self-confident that you really are. What's more, starting off a conversation with a compliment is a great way to naturally segue into an additional small talk. It is also important that you consider the version of yourself that you are presenting to the world. When someone is self-confident, other people tend to see them as outgoing, friendly and happy. Thus, you can reverse engineer the same results by making it a point to be all three to those you meet on a regular basis.

For starters, you are going to want to always introduce yourself to others before they have the chance to do the same, and also smiling more. Introducing yourself tells the other person that you have self-respect and thus you deserve their respect as well. Furthermore, you are going to want to fully commit yourself to any group activities that you find yourself a part of, and don't shy away from participating in group discussion as well. When you do speak, make it a point to avoid filler words such as like or um, words like these make it seem as though you aren't sure what you are going to say next or that you are uncertain of the point you are trying to make. Taken as a whole, these activities will naturally make you seem like someone who is more self-confident.

5

How to Cope with BPD with 5 STEPS to Balanced Responses

Now, this is a simple coping technique that has been a positive way to help people with a form of Cognitive Behavior Therapy. You have to know that if you want these steps to help you have to do more than just knowing them, you have to apply them. Changes won't happen overnight but if you keep at it and it becomes a normal thing for you then it can do wonders. I have confidence that if anyone puts their mind to it and actually uses it practically every day, they can change. But that will take every day having patience, giving time, and just practicing.

You will not master this right away so don't give up. I know it will be challenging but don't expect to master them right away. If you don't do so good one day then all you need to do is get back up on that horse and ride one, try harder next time and I know it will go better. Even if you aren't at the stage you want to be yet, it will be better than the last. Once you work these steps into your hindsight or even retrospectively will help you, but I can say even if you practice this for years or even practice this for decades you can be halted by your pie under desires. You have to remember all of the years of your old behaviors you are trying to change, it is going to be a process.

First, whenever you are feeling your feelings coming in you need to stop in your place. Just breathe for a second and try to analyze your feelings. Is it because you are angry? Maybe you are angry over a certain situation. Could you be feeling lonely at the moment? Maybe you are possibly just tired and needing a break from everything to sleep. You need to analyze yourself and see what you are feeling. You need to remember that whatever you are feeling is very physical and will always be temporary. Always remember that whatever you are feeling is in that moment. You don't always have to give in to every emotion, once you realize that in a day or two that this feeling on the inside is temporary you will be glad you kept it in instead letting it out all over your closest relationships.

Second, just figure out what the problem is. Figure out why you are feeling the way that you are feeling and what might have caused it. You might even come up with more than one problem at the moment, but whatever you find is annoying you should be written down on a piece of paper. Once you can centralize the problem you can start working past it or overcoming it. It becomes easier once you start figuring out your r own thoughts and why they come and go. The problem might not be super clear, you could just be filled with emotions and that's okay. Just don't feed into those emotions when you should remember that they are only temporary.

Third, you need to focus on your problems and try to work past them. The best way is when you write down every problem you should come up with three different solutions on how to fix it. You don't need ten and you can't have just one. You need choice in your life, and when every choice is given by yourself it makes it easier to make a decision. Every path in life always separates into smaller paths so you should know that every decision isn't going to be a straightforward solution. Some solutions work for some and not for others, that is why you need to be in control of your own self. I know you can do it because once you do I swear it feels like your high in the clouds.

Fourth, you should take some time to go over those options and make a choice. This choice doesn't have to be permanent, you can always try going a new route. If you pick something and go for it then you are the god of your own universe. If it doesn't end up working the way you thought it would, then don't get emotional at all. You can always rework the system and follow the steps again and try a new path. Even trying the other two ideas if you wanted would help you get down the path.

Fifth, you honestly just need to do it all! If you are reading this then that means you are still on this planet, it means you have survived with yourself for this long so you can go so much further. Nothing will change your own problem or issue you are experiencing until you do something about it. It doesn't have to fix the problem completely, even small acts towards yourself will help you. You can't go forward or backward until you start moving so just believe in yourself and try hard to go forward. To change your perspective or outlook on a situation you would have to change a little part of your inner self. You need to have that change be set in stone for when you want the outside world to see it because that is the only way to change the effect on how they see you is to keep it for a long time. You can't try for a day because people won't see the change in you, they can't tell the difference in that short amount of time.

If you are wanting to try these steps to help yourself get ahead in life, then first try with an old problem that has been bugging you. Maybe even a recent situation that has happened. You want to practice on this not spur of the moment so you know how to use these to your advantage. Always be checking your halt, your first step to having a balanced response. If you can check in with your emotions and actually understand them, then you can escalate to a positive point in your life. Once your conscious and subconscious kick in and realize there are better ways to deal with all of these stressful situations, you can apply the full five-step approach with ease. Everything in life that's good takes time, I truly believe you have it in you to give yourself this time. In a few years, you would be happy that you can analyze your situations and not just explode all over everyone that comes near you.

6 How to Accept Yourself and Add on Positive Effects

The first thing you have to understand is that no one hates you as much as you hate yourself. You need to ease up and relax about yourself, find the parts you enjoy and help them grow. I understand that people don't want to express themselves because they are always worried that others will judge them if they knew who they really were. But you have to realize that people won't reject you, and the ones that do are horrible people so you don't need them in your life.

There are pure people and people who take advantage, you need to be around those pure people because they will show you a new side of yourself. You can raise your confidence and no be scared of rejection. The only thing you would need to apply is the self-realization of your emotions. You need to be aware and hold back when you can. You can grow positive relationships this way and people could actually love you for just the person you always are.

Self-acceptance can be a magical thing when you have a borderline personality disorder because it allows you to feel that love and see it while right infant of the face of abandonment. You will learn to love others with their own flaws like they have learned to love yours. You can see the world is all so internally focused on their cracks in their personality that you aren't different at all. You will start to love yourself in the healthiest of ways and be more positive about yourself. It takes away that need to find acceptance through doing risky behavior. It helps you when those suicidal thoughts come and you can just shut them down. It helps you realize when your moods aren't stable and you need to find the balance. It also shows you when your mood is balled and you can see the serine pleasure of the calmness.

When you become unstable your more aware of the feeling, it doesn't just open the floodgates. You will finally feel like a whole person, someone who can fulfill their dreams. You will see yourself getting angry less of the time and it will become more of an uncommon thought that flows through your mind. You won't have to live afraid anymore, you can be yourself and be confident in who you are. The more confident you are the more people will come, and they hopefully will be positive experiences in your life instead of past negative relationships.

To see all of your good, you have to focus on your strengths inside. You can feed those to be stronger and while you are doing them, you can feed your insecurities. Everyone has them so you should be proud of what you have, the more open you are to others about yourself internally, but in a positive way, the better people will understand what you are going through. You don't have to feel so alone all of the time. There are people in the world who just like to help. There are people who always will speak negatively towards you and they are the people who just like to hurt you or push you down.

You don't need to deal with those types of people forever, the sooner you cut off every toxic relationship the better you will feel. If you can cut them off then you should try to fix it by learning more about yourself or going to couple's therapy. You can always fix relationships but some cannot be repaired because the people on the other side are not willing to change their awful ways. You need to find those people who make you feel great and create a support system out of them. You can't just lean one person, so having system would be ideal. The people that are accepting of who you are no matter what you have done and believe you can still go up from here are the ones you need.

Take to them first before you mentally put them in a category of people you can fall back on. Some can't take the responsibility or they kindly don't want to, that is okay because they are still a friend you can talk to when you are hanging out with them. You should have a few people that when something happens you can just call them or see them so you don't have a meltdown. People who like doing this for you exist, so get out of your negative canon and find these people.

The more negativity you surround yourself in the more you are going to feel suffocated. You shouldn't beat yourself up for anything in the past. If you can't even forgive yourself then why would you assume that others would do it for you? You will always have regrets but if all you are doing is examining those regrets you will never be able to practice your acceptance. You should forgive yourself as soon as it happens and move on. You shouldn't just forget about it though, you need to learn from it. That is how you grow as a human.

We all have tons of flaws and if we looked back in every bad decision we made then we would never go forward as a human race. You made your best decision with the information you had up available to you at the time. You can't beat yourself up about it because it's a memory. You are going to miss out on the greatness of the now if you are always focusing on the past.

A reason why you might beat yourself up all the time is the inner critic you have inside. It's the voice that is always showing you the insecurities and judgment. Some think of this voice as their internal voice of reason, so they are always listening to it. Do not feed into your internal harsh critic that we all have. You can start to quiet that voice by calming down and telling it that I am only human, I am doing all I can do. Failures are opportunities for a new way of learning and growth. Always speak to the highest version of yourself, the best version of you. That is who you want to talk to because the more you converse with it the more it will be brought out into your external image.

7

Awareness of Crisis Situations

It is very hard to open your mind if you don't have BPD to a crisis situation because you have never experienced it. Those moments of pure happiness or furious anger are your strongest moments, for someone with borderline personality disorder those emotions are like their normal day to day emotions. Crisis attacks are about ten times as intense as those normal emotions. It is hard to control, especially the farther you get into the crisis. You can always prevent it from happening if you think about your words before you say them. You should analyze all that you say and then you can say it, you don't have to be bluntly negative all the time.

To start to be aware of your crisis you might get a chemical change inside your body, that could be making you shake or making you irrational. That is your body getting ready for the crisis and expressing itself before you let it out. You will also get all of this anger and these thoughts flowing into your mind, your goal is to not catch a single one. You should let them go in one ear and out the other. Don't feed the bear, just be nice and polite with your conversations. What you give out to people is hopefully what you revive back from them, and the more positive it all is the more the positivity flows through you. If you can't hold back then just try to distract yourself with something, it could be reading your favorite book, watching a comedy, or even just going straight to the computer and typing out all of your feelings onto all of those pages. It just helps ease your feelings inside and help you get back to your normal levels. Anything you can do to go back to your normal levels is a good idea because the more you practice getting to that point the more easy and painless it will be to get there. Just believe in yourself, and that you can do it. If you need an extra push with support or therapy then take it because I know you can always be a better you. We all can. The effort you put in is the effort that comes back, so if you try to get better and stick to it for months or years and put in effort, you will see a return. You will always feel these symptoms during a crisis situation but over time they can get smaller and smaller, easier and easier to handle. Time is the key intros one, and the lock will take a lot of patience.

If you are in a crisis situation and none of your security web is there to talk to then there are still other options for you so you don't have to have an emotional event. 1-800-SUICIDE is always available to talk to you if you get to that dire state of your mind. They can be reached 24 hours a day because they genuinely care about people like you. They want to be there for you so nothing happens to you. You are very special and you don't realize it sometimes, especially when you are younger. There is also the Alcohol and Drug Information and Referral Service, which is if you are having a negative induced by that. It is available to anyone and you can call this number if you are concerned about a loved one with abuse. The number is 604-660-9382 and they are available like the suicide line all 24 hours of the day. The people on the other side of the phone genuinely want to hear what is upsetting you and how they can help you move past it. One more number you can call is 811, they are there for anything. You can call for any nonemergency health information, that includes all mental health information. You can also call this number to speak to a registered nurse if you are worried about any symptoms you have. If you have medicine questions then you can talk to a pharmacist as well.

There are many paths to take when you are in the moment, but you need to train yourself over time which paths are good to go down and which ones you should try to avoid. You are in control of everything you say and so you can make the situation less anger filled and more pleasure filled. You want to come out with a problem but do it in an approachable way that isn't harsh or demanding. You can practice how to do this in your free time with past reasons you got mad and how you could have handled it better. You are going to practice a lot because this won't just come naturally to you. But I believe you can do anything you set your mind to. Just watch out because you might have some anger slips at the beginning of your training, but after a few months, you will start to get in this new groove. It will be a very, very hard goal to get to but it will help take a strain off of your relationships, your job, your everyday life, and so much more. The sooner you start to apply this the sooner you will get results. I believe that any person at any age can do this, but it will get harder the older you get. When you start this change, you have to remember that you have been in this awful mindset your whole life.

You have to change your old habits and it will take years and years to cover these habits. Once you can control your emotions and your inner love towards yourself you will feel like a new man. Don't expect all of your symptoms to ever go away, you will always have them but at the end of your training, they will be reduced immensely. You will not be triggered as fast or as often.

Additionally, you will likely feel better if you institute a safety plan that you can rely on when you find yourself in the midst of suicidal thoughts or another type of high-risk behavior. Without this type of plan, you may end up in a situation where you are in danger of hurting yourself or someone else. Having a plan in place in case everything goes wrong will make it more difficult for you to take an action in the heat of the moment that you will possibly regret for the rest of your life. Additionally, it is important to keep in mind that the plan creation tips below can only be utilized properly when you or a loved one are in full control of their cognitive facilities, not when they are in the midst of serious crisis.

The first thing you are going to need to do is to talk to a professional about the ideas you have for your safety plan. Depending on your specific situation, they may recommend several different things, such as including or removing specific aspects based on your personalized needs. If you do not currently have someone who can work on a safety plan with you, it is important that you find a professional to talk with right away. If it is the stigma of seeing a therapist that is keeping you away, it is important to persevere, therapy was literally created for people in your situation.

Once you have spoken to a therapist, you will need their help when it comes to evaluating your potential dangers and risks including things such as suicidal thoughts, urges of violence, or thoughts of harming others no matter how fleeting they may be. Issues such as these are all going to be the primary target of your safety plan so it is crucial that you sit down and take the time to think things through before you discuss your issues with your therapist so that your ultimate plans end up working out as fully as possible.

In addition to helping you evaluate your current risk level, it is also important to keep in mind various factors in your life that may be escalating any of those potential dangers such as improper medication use or unhealthy relationships. If you own a weapon and depending on your situation, your healthcare provider may recommend turning the weapon over to the authorities for everyone's safety.

Once you know what the symptoms and behaviors you need to deal with are, you will be ready to start looking for their sources by identifying triggers. As an example, it is common for those who suffer from BPD to have issues dealing with abandonment which can lead to either real or imagined slight in this regard to be extremely troubling to deal with. If you understand that you have issues in this regard you can then be more aware of your triggers and what you can do in order to ensure they crop up as infrequently as possible.

In order to determine your triggers, the first thing you are going to want to do is to find a private place to record your thoughts. It is important to be aware that this exercise could potentially cause you distress, simply because you will be thinking about a lot of specific situations that are tied directly to your symptoms so you are going to want to be in a private place where you can plan for some soothing afterward.

Take a piece of paper and draw three columns on it. The first should be labeled trigger, the second emotion and the third response to emotion. You will then want to take some time and consider the last time you experienced an extremely negative emotional response. This could be something like emptiness, shame, sadness, fear, loneliness or anger. In the trigger column, you will want to write down the event that triggers the emotional response you remember, being as specific and detailed as you need to be. Remember, the goal here is to catalog issues to be avoided in the future so the more specific you can be about your triggers the better.

Additionally, when you are searching your memory for triggers, keep in mind that this could be either something internal or something external. It could be something obvious such as a fight you had with a loved one or it could simply be a depressing stray thought. When listing your triggers, it is important to examine the situation that spawned the response from every angle, it is possible that what you first consider the obvious trigger could actually be an ancillary part of the story. Find the true root triggers of your emotions for the best success.

Perhaps the most common triggers for BPD have something to do with interpersonal relationships. It is common for those with

BPD to experience thoughts of suicide, self-harm, anger, fear or other impulsive behavior after situations occur that lead to them feeling either abandoned, criticized or rejected. For example, it is likely that when you call a friend and they don't call you back you will likely have a series of spiraling thoughts about why your friend no longer likes you, why they are not calling you back and what it means for your friendship. This, in turn, leads to feelings of anger, sadness or an urge for self-harm.

Some individuals with BPD experience triggers that come in the form thoughts that appear as if from nowhere. This is especially true for those who experienced extreme forms of trauma when they were younger as intense emotions related to feelings from those times can often trigger the symptoms of BPD. This memory doesn't necessarily need to be all that distressing in and of itself either, happy memories can also lead to feelings that things are not as good now as they once were which can cause a spiral into depression.

When it comes to the emotion column you are going to want to fill in the emotional response you had to the trigger in question. It is important to not limit yourself to a single emotion per trigger as it is perfectly natural to feel multiple things once a trigger occurs. However, it is important to not force an emotional label on a specific trigger, if you can't determine exactly what you felt in the moment, it is better to leave the space blank than to incorrectly categorize the trigger. With this in mind, it is also important that you don't avoid listing emotions because you don't want to deal with the consequences of doing so, the purpose of the exercise is to improve in the long run after all, which makes the difficulty more than worth it.

In the final column, you are going to write down the way you responded to the feelings that the trigger caused. As an example, if you felt extremely ashamed because of a specific trigger then the action may be self-harm. The situations you list don't all have to be negative, however, as there is a benefit to being able to see, written out in front of you, the things you did right as well. For example, you could have gotten angry after a specific trigger but perhaps you used coping skills as a means of managing that anger effectively. Once you have successfully determined your list of triggers, you may find it helpful to revisit your list on a regular basis, if only to see how far you have come.

With the list in front of you, you are going to want to look at the triggers column and determine if you can see any patterns developing there. In general, most people will be able to determine a few different primary categories that their triggers are grouped around. One common grouping of triggers for people with BPD is a perceived sense of rejection. While eventually, you will discover most if not all of your triggers, during the early days you are going to want to keep it with you and add to it every time something list-worthy happens throughout your day. Keeping the list on you will also make you more aware of moments where your triggers have come into play, hopefully making it easier for you to resist giving into the negative response in time.

Once you are aware of your triggers, you will be able to get to work on avoiding them, some of which are going to be easier to avoid than others. Likewise, some triggers will be impossible to avoid, while still others will be better for you to deal with face to face. Overall, avoidance is a strategy that should be used as sparingly as possible. It is better to make coping with issues part of your plan as opposed to simply avoiding them as you will then have no plan in place for when the avoidance plan fails.

Instead, a good option is to approach scenarios where you feel you will have to come face to face with your triggers in a strategic fashion. While productive, this method can be stressful and it is recommended that you proceed with the help of a therapist. When you are first getting started it is best to work with a small trigger so that you can face it in a controlled and limited way.

As an example, if you find that the idea of failure is one of your biggest triggers, then you can face it in a small way first, such as by trying a yoga pose that you know you are unable to do. Make a point of trying this pose regularly, and then when you fail you can be aware of the various physical and emotional responses you are feeling so you can start dealing with them in a more positive way. Rather than feeling disappointed or rejected, you may find that you can cope in a more positive way possible through meditation or maybe even just by laughing at yourself. The specifics don't matter, all that really does is that you learn to face the idea of failing without resorting to behavior that is destructive to yourself or others.

If you feel as though your triggers typically send you into an emotional loop you can't seem to break free from, try writing down a handful of things you can do to manage your emotions and break yourself out of the cycle the next time you experience a trigger. You can then keep this list on you at all times, you will be surprised at how just having the list on you can help prevent you from ending up in a destructive loop. When the trigger does occur, don't hesitate, pull out the list and try what you have written down, if the first one doesn't work then go onto the next and then the next. Go through the whole list, multiple times if needed, whatever you need to free yourself from the loop. Knowing you have an out when it comes to a particularly aggressive trigger will often go a long way towards making it feel more manageable which will often prevent it from triggering anything at all.

When working on your safety plan, you are going to primarily want to focus on the triggers that have the biggest potential of leading you to harm yourself or others as the goal should be to keep you as safe as possible. You can think of these as resources to help you cope that you can use before your symptoms get so severe that you end up in a full-blown mental health crisis.

Now that your plan is coming together you are going to want to commit it to paper. You should have a list of your riskiest behaviors, their triggers, plans for coping when things get out of hand along with ways to respond in case you find yourself in an emergency scenario. You will then want to put all of these together to ensure that you have a reliable, step by step plan of action ready to go in case you really need it. While it is a lot of work up front, as soon as you use it for the first time you will realize just how worth it all the effort was.

With each behavior, you are going to want to write out the issues that trigger it, several useful coping responses that can get you out of the mental loop the trigger causes, what to do if they don't work and how to avoid an impending emergency situation. Once you have a list of all the risks you need to keep in mind, and how you will deal with them, the last thing you will need to do is to make a promise to yourself to stick to your safety plan as much as possible, and mean it. Making a conscious choice, when you are in a reliable mental state will make it easier to not think and just follow the outlined steps when you need them the most. Waiting to commit can lead to situations where you lose your resolve in the moment, which can shove all the hard work and planning you did down the drain.

Depending on your personal situation, your therapist might even recommend having you sign the plan.

8

Cutting Edge Treatments and Cures

People with BPD need to find a way to just cope with how they are internally. It helps having someone there to guide them along. The main treatment that is provided for people with borderline personality disorder is using psychotherapy. Some can have medication as well or even hospitalization with the therapy. Treating your disorder instead of just ignoring it can make you feel so much more positive towards yourself and just live a more structured life, it gets rewarding once you have given it the time it needs. You can't expect overnight changes, you are going to have to put in the effort to become a more stable you.

The first path that you can take with BPD is doing psychotherapy. It has another name of talk therapy and is a very common treatment towards borderline personality disorder. Your therapist will then be comfortable with your BPD and already be acquainted with the disorder. They can also shape your therapy around your own personal needs and growths. Psychotherapists only are there to help you, they understand what you are going through and hey will come towards you with the least aggressive perception of your reality. They will help if you let them in and give effort back.

Psychotherapists are there to meet the needs you are wanting to achieve, they will do a lot to help. They are analyzing your ability to function in the moment and see how much it can improve. Also, you will be at least slightly able to control your own emotions, especially taking comfortably to an unknown person. They are there to focus on your feelings with you and analyze them so you can reduce your impulsivity and control your actions from the feelings. You should also learn how to bring up your relationships to a nice level by being completely aware of how you are expressing your emotions and how they are doing the same. Obviously, they will overall just inform you about borderline personality disorder. You might know a lot about it but they will fill in those cracks that will help keep your human structure together. It is worth having a second perspective on your life when you know that they are only there to help. They won't leave you until you are on the right track and they will be supportive just like you have needed for your whole life.

If you are in any way curious of psychotherapy then you could research the subcategories of the therapy. There will always be new technologies available and new treatments out there so here are six different therapies that I can suggest. First, you could take Dialectical behavior therapy in a group setting or individual setting. This therapy is specifically targeted towards people with borderline personality disorder. It is more based on skills to teach you in a comfortable way. It teaches you how to maintain your emotions, deal with internal stress, and improve the quality of every relationship.

Another way you can be treated is with Schema-Focused therapy. As like Dialectical behavior therapy, you can talk this in a group setting or you can do it in an in-divide setting. It will help you face your unmet needs and desires deep down that have led you down the path you have taken. It could have caused bad patterns in life that can be a problem when you are an adult. Those experiences can hurt many parts of your life and daily life. This therapy mainly focuses on your life path and helping you walk down it in a brighter light. All that they want to see is you starting a life pattern that is just completely positive. The third choice would be Metallization-based therapy, which is a type of talk therapy. It helps you to express yourself any unknown or known internal thoughts and feelings. It helps you create a different perspective on your situation but still through your own eyes. You will understand why you are feeling the way you are from seeing it in a whole new way.

Mentalization-based therapy is going to be all about thinking before you apply the action. There is also the System training for emotional predictability and problem-solving, STEPPS is the acronym. It is a treatment that you would have to dedicate yourself to, it is a process. It takes 20 weeks to complete and you work in a group setting. You are in groups that are with your loved ones, caregivers, close friends, or spouses. This psychotherapy is used in correlation to any other of these therapies. It helps them apply what they are learning as they are learning it. It also helps your close family and friends to see what you are actually going through.

Next, we have Transference-focused psychotherapy which is also called psychodynamic psychotherapy. It is there to help you understand your emotions and internal struggles with a one on one connection you grow with your therapist. They will help mold your brain to open your eyes to all sides of you. They want to help you get on the right path so you should apply everything you hear in your therapy sessions out in your real life. Lastly, there is General psychiatric management. This therapy is about finding yourself internally and passing all the conflicts as well as dealing with your outer emotions. It is a common therapy and it is usually conjoined with medicine, group therapies, family education on BPD, and more individual therapies.

If you are wanting to make the path of medicine, then there is some good and bad. There is the medicine that can help, but not completely. There have been no drugs approved yet by the FDA that is specifically used as a treatment for borderline personality disorder. There are certain medications out there that can help with your symptoms or reoccurring problems like anxiety, aggression, depression, and impulsivity.

These medications could be in the classes of antidepressants, antipsychotics, or even just mood stabilizing drugs. The one person who will definitely know what is best for you to take is your primary care provider. They will know what symptoms you needed relieved and they could give you the best option, or even if they think medicine is a good option. There will be side effects from some so you should have caution if you are curious about this step.

In a small chance that you need a firmer treatment than therapy, you can go to a hospital or clinic that specializes in psychiatric help. This can be a positive place to be especially if you have had thoughts or actions of self-inflicted injury or suicide. You will be under care for a long time there, not just an appointment. It is a hard step for some people to take but others really need this push to start seeing themselves in a different light.

Always remember that learning all of these treatments of expressing and understanding your inner self and external words will never happen easy. You are going have to work for it, but if you have come this far in life then I know you can handle this challenge. It takes a long time to reverse how you have been living for all of this time. Be patient because it will come. Your thoughts and behaviors will take time until they become a subconscious act to be positive. You might have to wait months or even years to see the outcome and stick with therapy the whole ride. You won't ever get completely cured, you will just learn how to deal with it better and control it. Years after, you could still struggle with a few of your symptoms but just give it time. You will always go through waves of your symptoms coming and going, control those emotions and you can feel better about yourself.

9

Building Relationships

People who experience borderline personality disorder have a hard time developing relationships and keeping them stable. It is hard to get personally connected with others with the way they express their emotions. But it is very hard for people with BPD to be alone, they are stuck in their head and stuck thinking about abandonment issues. All of that just keeps adding to the anxiety. People with BPD have a hard time easing their anger and also like to undermine their spouse. You can barely see this process because people like to mask their dependence towards someone and manipulation. They have an unstable view of their own self, which leads to impulse decisions and very demanding confrontations.

It's a sad cycle of love and relationships for people with BPD. But don't think this of all relationships, some can get passed this cycle People with BPD usually abuse something like substances and it creates conflict. You are wanting that connection but still fighting with them like a child. Most partners will have this conflict and if they cannot work past it can come to divorce and even domestic violence. Reasons like these with relationships is why people with BPD have a very hard time giving their trust to others.

You need people around your life that are like a sponge to your emotions and won't break from what you say. It is very common to have wrongful anger and many breakdowns with the people that are close in your life. It's not because you don't care for them, it's actually the opposite. Most symptoms of borderline personality disorder are equivalent to love addiction. Now, this isn't an actual diagnosis but you can see it within people with addictive behavior. You can see this in others by how past their relationships grow and how passionate it is right out of the gate.

People with BPD cannot see the issues in their partner and don't have a very open mind to intimacy changes. No matter how great your partner is, they will disappoint you in one way or another because they will always conceive it in their black and white thought pattern. It might not have been put off in the way you received it. You need to learn how to responsibly deal with your emotions, especially towards the ones you love.

There was a study done that showed people with borderline personality disorder showing they actually have a different sense of every social norm, so it impacts their mind and ability to give trust or listen while cooperating. When a relationship has something go wrong, people with BPD do not respond in a way to fix the issue. That causes the significant other to not want to fully cooperate with him in the future. People with BPD can hardly get passed their own emotional screen to look at what others are going through.

They are so opus on themselves because just seeing their emotions and dealing with them is a huge hurdle. Especially in women, research shows that people experiencing borderline personality disorder have problems with sexual attitude and patterns of very unstable relationships. They use sexuality as a way to avoid the emptiness experienced inside and helps with tampering your anxiety you have felt during previous abandonment.

People experiencing BPD do not think in the way that they are ever satisfied emotionally. They can definitely still give out their needs emotionally in a positive healthy way. But, as soon as they aren't getting what they want from the connection then the anger and frustration come back. Inside there is an intense fear of being lonely and being abandoned but on the outside, the individual just feels pure anger. Some people diagnosed with borderline personality disorder can't comprehend how to control their rage and anger, so some take it to a physical level with their significant other. Studies done have shown that people with BPD are related to being aggressive towards your partner, physically, emotionally, and sexually they are showing their internal anger.

People with BPD really see the world as either everyone is good or everyone is bad. They see the world as a negative place with horrible people or this place where everyone is just trying to live their own life and be grateful that they are still here in this moment. With that perspective that really will change the relationship with your significant other. IF you see all as bad then you will see the negative in your spouse a lot easier than most.

It becomes hard when you are the spouse of someone with BPD. You will want to leave but without realizing it they are using their own manipulation to keep them around. Studies show that men are more emotionally intense than women with borderline personality disorder. They show an increase of jealousy, anger, and depression which are common in these men. But you need to remember that it's not all men with BPD. Some can also be aggressive if they think there is a gap or void in a relationship that doesn't need to be there.

The best thing you can do to start going up in your relationship is counseling and therapy. It sounds like a lot, but if you truly want this person in your life for a long time then you are going to need to put some effort into the relationship. You both can seek different therapists or they can try a conjoined therapy session. Just taking this step is a huge vital step into truly understanding your significant other with borderline personality disorder. If you worked with different therapists first then you could both work on your individual issues before diving into the relationship. Since the rise of supply and demand with BPD counseling, there are plenty therapists out in the world who specialize with BPD patients. Those are the people worth going to because they can teach you more about yourself or if your significant other had BPD they can teach you so much about the disorder.

If you are in a relationship with someone with BPD please go to counseling or just research borderline personality disorder so you can try your hardest to understand what your spouse is going through. It is a hard path but starting with the first step is all you need to worry about.

If pure counseling or therapy doesn't work for yourself or your significant other than you can try numerous options to help. You can go into hospitalization for as long as needed to completely learn about yourself. You could research hospitals that even are drug-free or your religion, you can go anywhere, it doesn't have to be like the movies. If the drug route is your way then you could talk to your therapist about what medications could work for you. Medicine helps balance out your internal chemical wheel and can definitely work for some people. If drugs are part of the reason you are going down in the relationship or in life then you can try substance abuse treatment.

You can learn about how to function without those extra additives in life. You can help become a purer version of you, your child state form of yourself. They even have support groups for your loved ones to take if they wanted to. Those can help you understand that you aren't alone with this and you can expand your knowledge on the subject of borderline personality disorder.

10

Stories About People with BPD That Overcome It All

There are many different types of people that have BPD and most react differently to situations. Some people overcome the disorder and can still live normal lives that some people probably would never tell that they had BPD. Now there are others, who can't cope with their disorder and they let it take them over. Most people are like this within the slightest during their first stages of diagnosis. You don't really understand why you are the way that you are, but you will slowly understand it and overcome your situation. So many people in the past have had BPD and they are still here within their own stories to tell us what they did to overcome it all. It is a song challenge for yourself, but once you have accepted it and started working towards a better you then you will see the progress. I swear in the end its worth it to grab a hold of your disorder so you are in control, not the other way around.

If you are a loved one or a friend than this story is meant to help you. It isn't just about the person with BPD because all of the family has to be around them all the time, so you should learn how to deal with your family member so you can be more aware. Just like this man and his BPD wife.

She had BPD and it made her fall into a downward spiral. There were countless police charges and suicide attempts, so that included many institutional visits. Her husband tried following her around like a pet just trying to help wherever he can, but he realized too far in that he was trying to help in all the wrong ways. He was always trying to help her, not focusing on the pain that he and his 3 kids were going through. He didn't realize that she is the only one who can really help herself and she needs to figure out this part of her life on her own. Then he finally just looked at himself, instead of just focusing on the BPD he saw himself. He realized that this is almost as hard on him as a wife. He started to go to non-BPD therapies and express his emotions on the matter. He always wondered why he should put up with this abuse, what he should do to help his kids not suffer, and slowly seeing his life die infant of his eyes. Therapy was the best decision in the world, it helped this man regain some of his strength that he had lost before.

He stood up to his wife and told her either he leaves with the kids or she leaves for extensive therapy. He took a bold move because he genuinely cares about this relationship. You can see that she does too and she did not want to get a divorce, so she went off to a 16-week therapy. That therapy was DBT and CBT based, with no drugs given at all. In that time period, her husband worked on himself and realized all the things he was doing to "help" her that was eventually "hurting" her. To this day, when she comes back from therapy, their whole family is stronger for it. They were all happy because they knew how well she did at therapy. There's obviously still going to be some moments, but they never escalate past that. That was one of the main issues of before. The moral of the story is to always work on yourself, always accept what is coming to you, give everyone a choice, and stand your ground. Good luck to you all.

If you are one of many people in this world and you have Borderline Personality Disorder, the first step you are taking to research is outstanding. Learning about your disorder will not happen overnight, like any other subject there are just too many branches that come off of the truck. You can start to learn about something and then realize that it just goes deeper and deeper into the subject. It will take some time, probably years, but you will find yourself at the end of all of this. You just really need to have the desire to do it. Here's a story of a man who successfully overcame his disorder, just some inspiration to everyone reading this.

You have to remember before reading this story that your problems aren't going to magically go away. The more success stories you read the more you come to the fact that this all shouldn't be so linear. No matter where you are in your stage of accepting yourself you will always have ups and downs. At the end stage of your acceptance, you will still have those down moments. The struggle only just gets easier, but you have to remember that it will always be there. This man is in his mid-20's and diagnosed 7 years ago. The day he got diagnosed he rushed home to research literally every end of what he had.

This man became ecstatic because he now knew the explanation of all his problems. He thought maybe he wasn't a bad person or that things aren't always his fault like people told him countlessly and made him believe it. He finally saw his opening to get better, to be more like the rest. Sadly, a couple years later there was a social stigma around the world that having a mental illness is horrible. Everyone around him was saying he just hid behind his diagnosis and just used the disorder as an excuse for bad behavior. He ended up thinking that of himself because that's all he was getting out of people. In these moments, he thought about all the steps he has taken so far, and they all just meant nothing. It's like square one again. Every feeling of worthlessness and doubt came back in my mind full swing.

He quit his hobbies, he quit writing, and just though little of himself again.

It felt like he couldn't do anything to positively impact himself or his family because of what has happened in the past. Most of his family members don't believe in his diagnosis and his friends all eventually end up leaving because of short moments of time where he wasn't in control of his emotions. I never blamed anyone for not wanting to be near or around me, but not having a support system was breaking him. Even though he lives at his father's house, he barely speaks to him. He is just always scared of the awful words that will slip out of his mouth next. Every single part of his surroundings left him feeling like there was no hope because there was always no help. Nobody wanted a man like him in their life, someone with all these questionable actions in the past.

The turning point was when he ended up reading a book that overall taught him that there are actually good people in this world. It showed that some people always want to help, they are willing and even eager for the chance, and just that made him smile. He has to have frequent reminders of this because the people around and his internal self, are making him lose faith in all of the humanity and shatter all his hopes. All he wants is for people to show love in this world because humanity can be pretty beautiful if we all tried. Those strong emotions you feel when you first fall in love or when you are at the peak of your anger are wrong emotions that people with BPD have to deal with on a day to day basis.

Now if you take those emotions up 10 notches that that is what someone with BPD calls intense emotions. Your emotions can become unbearable fast because the BPD kicks in. You can't control your mind, your body, or your speech. It can take over and say or do things that you will end up regretting deeply but you will always have to live with it. People will assume it was your fault because that's what their perspective can see, they will never know how hard you fought to keep control. It's very easy to feel helpless and very hopeless, thinking there is nothing to completely fix you. You think of yourself as completely toxic and that is a very toxic thought to have about yourself. You need to control your emotions or you will be lead to damaged relationships, people walking away, and ends up causing you abandonment issues in the process. It is a cycle of negativity that only you can break.

The turning point to all of this is people around the world need to be aware of the words they say to anyone, especially people with mental illnesses, beach it is damaging and it sticks with a person. The people in this world that are aware and actually care are the ones you need in your life. You need pushes up in the world not down. He feels helpless but truly doesn't want the whole world to be in the same boat. All this man wants you to grab from this story is if you have

BPD then it's not your fault and there are people out there who are willing to be there for you, people who genuinely care about you.

If you don't have BPD and you are reading this, think before you speak. I know everyone reading this has some negative comment someone has said about you years and years ago, but can't remember who was the last person to say something nice to you. Fix the problem don't just be the problem. Some people in this world are genuine and some aren't, its sadly the way that the world turns. You can't have one without the other, but if you are surrounded by negativity all the time every day and you have BPD, I swear you should find new people and you will forever be, please.

You will still have your moments and your outbursts, but they can be contained to a minimal. Positive help and positive thinking can really make you go far with your lives journey. I believe that every single person who has BPD can make a better version of themselves that they can actually enjoy. You all are amazing human beings, it just matters if your watering and feeding the positivity plant or the negativity plant. It's always your choice.

CPSIA information can be obtained
at www.ICGtesting.com
Printed in the USA
LVHW030205200323
741997LV00013B/881